£2.80

THIS BOOK BELONGS TO...

Shayne Flower

...AND IT'S NOT FOR SAK SALE!

THE TOPPER BOOK — 1988

HOST TRAIN

Printed and Published in Great Britain by D.C. Thomson & Co., Ltd.,
185 Fleet Street, London, EC4A 2HS.

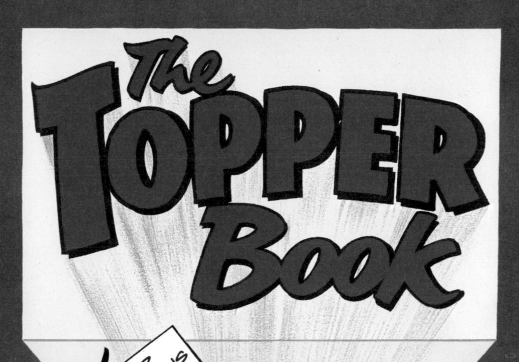

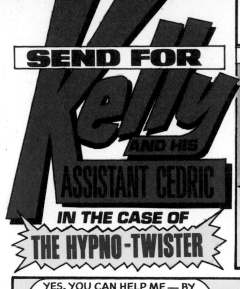

SEND FOR Kelly AND HIS ASSISTANT CEDRIC
IN THE CASE OF THE HYPNO-TWISTER

AT A BRANCH OF BOODLE'S BANK —

GOOD MORNING, SIR! CAN I HELP YOU?

YES, YOU CAN HELP ME — BY JUST LOOKING INTO MY EYES.

NOW FILL UP MY BAG WITH CASH — LOTS AND LOTS.

MY PLEASURE, SIR.

TIME FOR A SPEEDY GETAWAY! BY BUS — NO FUSS.

FARES, PLEASE.

FARES? WHAT A GOOD IDEA!

LOOK INTO MY EYES . . . KEEP LOOKING . . . YOU WILL NOW DO AS I SAY . . .

. . . EMPTY OUT YOUR BAG — 'COS I'M HAVING THE FARES. TA!

LATER —

THE MINISTER WANTS TO SEE US URGENTLY, MR KELLY. I WONDER WHY?

MINISTRY OF SECRET INFORMATION

MUST BE SOMETHING REALLY IMPORTANT.

FRESH FISH

IT CERTAINLY IS!

I'VE JUST BEEN ROBBED. THE BLIGHTER EVEN TOOK MY CLOTHES!

THE THIEF HYPNOTISED ME, SOMEHOW, THEN ORDERED ME TO HAND OVER EVERYTHING — SUIT AND ALL!

WE'LL LOOK INTO IT, MINISTER.

SO —

MARCO THE MESMERIST AT THE TOWN HALL TODAY

HMM! THIS COULD BE OUR CROOK. LET'S ATTEND HIS SHOW.

HERE HE COMES. SHUT YOUR EYES, CEDRIC. WE MUST MAKE SURE WE'RE NOT HYPNOTISED, OR WE WON'T KNOW WHAT'S GOING ON?

WELCOME, LADIES AND GENTLEMEN. I WANT YOU ALL TO LOOK CLOSELY INTO MY EYES.

KEEP LOOKING — YES — NOW YOU ARE IN MY POWER! KINDLY MAKE YOUR WAY OUT, HANDING ME YOUR CASH AND JEWELLERY AS YOU GO . . .

I WAS RIGHT, CEDRIC. MARVO IS A CROOK!

AS MARVO STARTS TO LEAVE WITH HIS LOOT, KELLY MAKES HIS MOVE . . .

MARVO! STOP WHERE YOU ARE, YOU THIEF. YOU'RE UNDER ARREST.

EXIT

ER — MR KELLY CAREFUL! HE MAY —

— HYPNOTISE US!

LOOK DEEPLY INTO MY EYES — DEEPLY! YOU'RE FALLING ASLEEP — DEEP, DEEP SLEEP.

HAND ME YOUR WALLETS, SUCKERS! HO! HO! HO!

SOON, WHEN THE HYPNOSIS WEARS OFF.

I'VE BEEN ROBBED.

ME, TOO! GOSH — WE NEED TO TAKE SPECIAL MEASURES IF WE'RE GOING TO ARREST THAT CRAFTY VILLAIN.

SO KELLY GOES TO PROFESSOR WRIGHT-NITT FOR ADVICE . . .

. . . YES, KELLY, OLD BEAN, THESE SPECIAL GOGGLES WILL STOP YOU BEING HYPNOTISED.

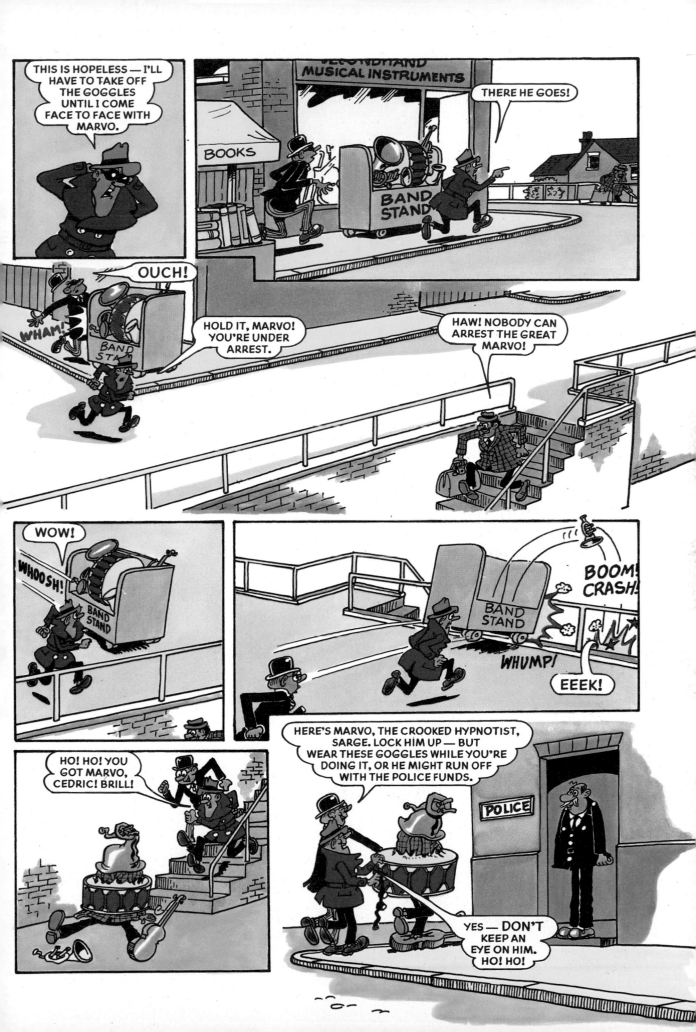

MARVELLOUS MASCOTS!

— SOME FAMOUS BIRDS AND BEASTS THAT WENT TO WAR!

During the First World War, a well-known British general had an unusual pet. It was a full-grown lion and its name was Poilu. Everyone except the general was scared stiff of the lion. But whenever anyone suggested that the animal should be removed to a zoo, the general would say— "Come and take him away, then!" Nobody dared go near Poilu, so the lion was allowed to remain with his master.

During the Battle of Britain, in 1940, a French fighter squadron had a duck for their mascot. They called their pet "Donald," and gave him the rank of corporal. Painted on the side of every plane in the squadron was a large-sized picture of Corporal Duck!

One of the biggest mascots of all must have been the elephant which once belonged to a battalion of the famous Scottish regiment, the Seaforth Highlanders. Jumbo was specially trained to lead the battalion pipe band on parade.

In the North African desert, during the last war, the 51st Highland Division had a strange mascot — a fat-tailed ram called Willie. He ate all sorts of queer things, including soap. When the Division took part in the invasion of Sicily, Willie went ashore, too!

AMMO

SOAP

When the 2nd Battalion of the Scots Guards captured two cows in Belgium, during the First World War, they "adopted" them as mascots, and called them Bella and Bertha. Because the two cows had so much walking to do, they were shod like horses. Bella and Bertha led the battalion in a parade in London in 1919.

The smallest paratrooper in the 1939-45 War was a little chap called Louis. He was a monkey from the Belgian Congo, and became the mascot of an Allied airborne company. When practice jumps were being made from aeroplanes, Louis took part in the training, too. He had a special small-sized parachute.

...ny years ago, when the British Army was fighting against the fierce Dervishes in the Sudan, they had a mascot called ...dy. Paddy was a fox-terrier, and in a battle at Suakin he showed his bravery by taking part in a charge against the ...my. He raced along, barking and snapping furiously at the natives' heels. For his valour, Paddy received a medal.

The crew of a British gun-boat in China adopted a young alligator which they named Algernon, who loved being hosed down with water, and scrubbed with a hard broom. But the sailors had to get rid of him because, later on, he used to sneak up on them and bowl them over with a swish of his tail!

This West African crested crane — the mascot of the 2nd Battalion the Queen's Own Nigerian Regiment — had a good view when the Duke of Gloucester made an inspection, during the Nigerian self-government celebrations.

BLAM!

YAAGH!

CHONK!

HOW'S THAT, F'R GETTING AHEAD? CACKLE!

LATER—

THERE YOU GO! TWO CORNETS F'R TWO CUSTOMERS!

AND ONE BALLOON . . .

TONY'S ICE CREAM

. . . FOR DOUBLE FUN!

BOOM!

YIKES!

SPLATCH!

SPLOTCH!

TONY'S ICE CREAM

GORPS!

AND ON SOME MORE—

I'LL JUST FINISH BLOWIN' UP THIS BALLOON I'VE HALF-FILLED WITH WATER . . .

A STAB-STAB HERE, AND A STAB-STAB THERE!

. . . AND PUT IT UNDER HERE.

FROOTLE! TOOTLE! TUTTLE! FRUTTLE!

HARFLE! WATER LAUGH!

BANG!

SOON, OUTSIDE THE LOCAL CONCERT CLUB—

...AND SO YEHUDI WILL NOW BEGIN...

YEHUDI MENUDI *Violinist* RECITAL TODAY

AND SO WILL I!

I'LL JUST LET THE AIR OUTA THE BALLOON SLOWLY.

SNIGGER!

SCRAAAW! SCREEECH! GRAAARN!

WOT A DIN!

EH?

RASP! GARBAGE!

YEUCH! HE'S SUPPOSED TO BE GOOD, TOO!

ON GOES BERYL—

THAT HAMBURGER PLACE LOOKS A GOOD SPOT F'R SOME MORE FUN.

HAMMY'S HAMBURGER BAR

INSIDE—

ACE!

DUCK!

FALL!

NONK!

SOON, BACK AT THE PARK—

REALLY **BIG** BALLOONS! BRILL! WHAT I WOULDN'T GIVE TO HAVE ONE OF **THEM**!

THEN—

EH? IT'S GONE ALL DARK!

BERYL'S GOT HER BIG BALLOON!

HULLO, BERYL!

WE'VE BEEN GETTING LOTS OF COMPLAINTS ABOUT YOUR BEHAVIOUR— SO WE ARRANGED THIS LITTLE SURPRISE.

OORF! MUM 'N' DAD! IN A BALLOON!

SLIPPER READY FOR YOU-KNOW-WHAT!

CRUMP!

ONE WHACKING LATER—

I'LL FILL BERYL'S LAST BALLOONS WITH LIGHTER-THAN-AIR GAS.

WELL, IT SHOULD HELP US GET HER HOME . . .

RECENTLY USED.

SSS!

. . . AFTER ALL, SHE SAID SHE WAS TOO SORE TO WALK, AFTER THAT KING-SIZED WHACKING!

OOH! MY SIT-ME-DOWN!

FLOAT!

TWIT!

DESERT ISLAND DICK

"TREASURE ISLAND" IS A GREAT STORY, OLLY.

OLLY, DICK'S CASTAWAY PAL.

I'LL PRETEND TO BE LONG JOHN SILVER.

ARR, JIM, LAD!

I AM NOT JIM LAD.

FIND THE TREASURE, JIM, LAD.

LET'S HAVE A PEEP AT THIS BOOK. AH, I SEE . . .

THESE FEATHERS AND OLD SCARF SHOULD DO THE TRICK.

HUP!

HEAVE-HO, ME HEARTIES!

WHAT ARE YOU DOING?

HO! HO! OLLY WANTS TO BE LONG JOHN SILVER'S PARROT!

PETER PIPER

♪ HIS MAGIC PIPES BRING THINGS TO LIFE

WE'VE BEEN INVITED TO COUSIN JIM'S WEDDING!

SUPER! PETER, YOU'LL NEED A NEW SHIRT!

BASIL'S BOUTIQUE

LATEST GEAR

I'LL GET IT MYSELF AND SAVE MUM THE EXPENSE.

HERE YOU ARE, PAL!

LATEST GEAR

HMM... IT'S A BIT BIG...

CINEMA

THE AMAZING SHRINKERS FROM OUTER SPACE

SHOWING ALL THIS WEEK

REX

AH! JUST THE JOB. I'LL BRING HIM TO LIFE WITH MY MAGIC PIPES.

OOGLE-DE-GOOP!

ZEEEEEEEP!

YIPPEE! IT'S WORKED.

HOW D'YOU LIKE MY NEW SHIRT FOR THE WEDDING, MUM?

EEK! YOU'RE NOT WEARING THAT!

WHIZZERS FROM OZZ

THE METEOR. HUH! WHAT A DAFT TITLE FOR AN ESSAY! I CAN'T THINK WHAT TO WRITE!

Willie Walker, of Workchester, England, was busy doing some holiday homework.

Then something happened to cheer up Willie — and give Willie's Dad the fright of his life!

YIKES!

GOSH! KRIK AND KRAK!

WHOOSH!

SORRY, PUSS!

The small space-craft that had shot down out of the sky contained two special chums of Willie's — twins Krik and Krak, from the land of Whizz, on the far-off planet of Ozz!

HI, WILLIE — WE'VE COME TO TAKE YOU TO SEE THE ANNUAL HISTORY PAGEANT ON OZZ!

WHOOPEE! I'LL JUST GO AND ASK MUM AND DAD FIRST.

A short while later, the amazing little Whizz-car was zooming through the emptiness of space.

Then, as Willie and the twins shot past an odd-looking greeny-blue planet — problems!

BETTER LAND ON THIS PLANET. I THINK METEOR DUST IS FOULING UP OUR STAR-DRIVE!

SPLUTT!

But —

OZZ-KORKS! WE'RE BEING ATTACKED — BY GHOSTS!

REPULSER NET — ON!

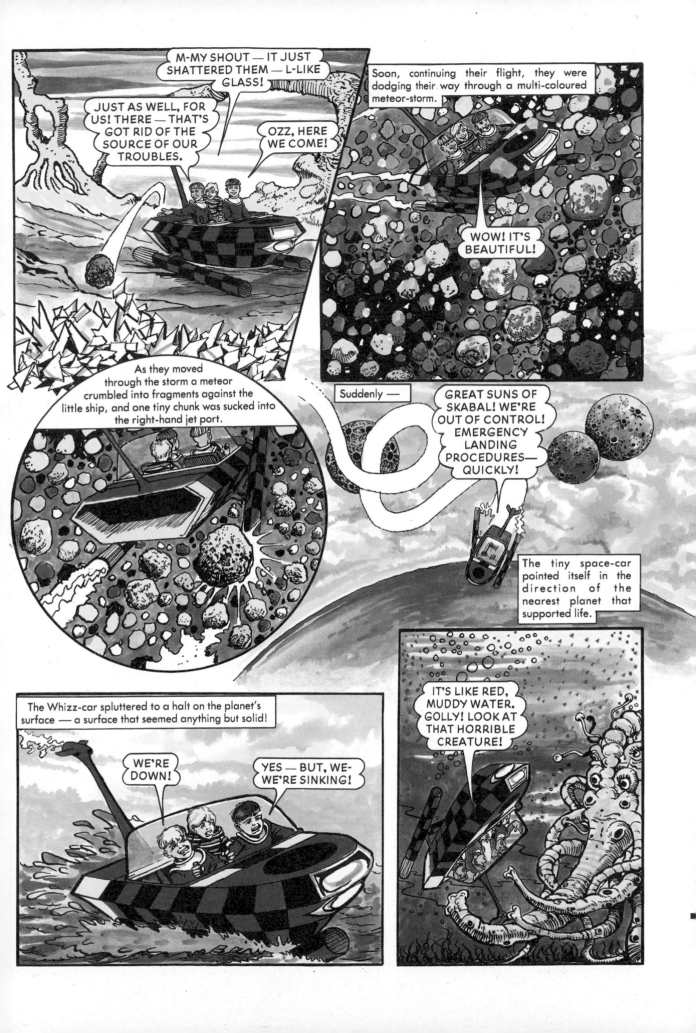

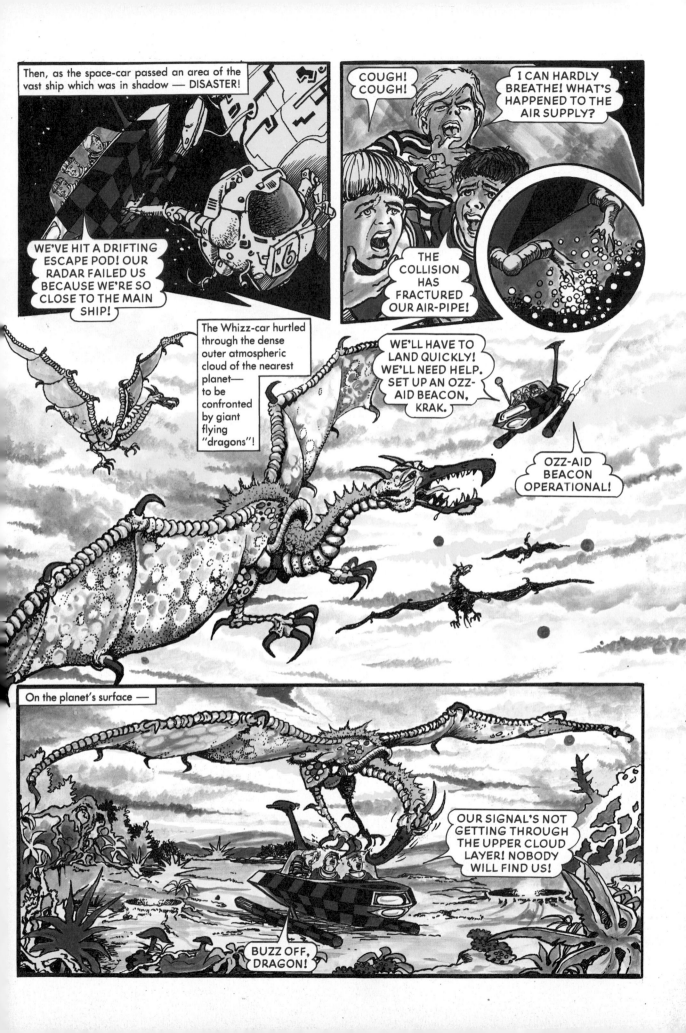

A couple of Ozz-days later, Willie was a relieved spectator at the Ozz History Pageant —

TRIFF! AMAZING! WONDERFUL! COO!

Safely delivered back on Earth at the end of his Ozz visit, Willie picked up a pen . . .

THANKS TO THAT TRIP, I THINK I CAN WRITE AN ESSAY ABOUT METEORS NOW.

After the school holidays, when Willie's teacher had read his essay —

THAT'S QUITE AN IMAGINATION YOU HAVE, WILLIE. WELL WRITTEN! BUT TOTALLY UNBELIEVABLE!

HEH! LITTLE DOES SHE KNOW!

A GROUP of GIGGLES!

You've heard of a FLEET of ships, a HERD of cows, a GAGGLE of geese. Now see some of the strange COLLECTIONS that our giddy artist has just invented.

PEARL

BERYL'S PERILOUS PET

WILLIE FIXIT

WOW! I WONDER WHAT IT'S LIKE TO RIDE A BUCKING BRONCO?

SID, I'LL FIX IT SO YOU FIND OUT! C'MON!

YOIPS! GREAT! BUT YOU COULD'VE WAITED TILL THE FILM WAS FINISHED!

I DON'T THINK THAT LITTLE SHETLAND PONY WILL RUN AWAY.

YEAH! MUCH SAFER.

COO! IT'S AWFUL DARK IN HERE. THINK I COULD DO WITH A HAIRCUT.

BAH! YOU'RE A WASH-OUT, FIXIT!

HOLD IT! I CAN STILL FIX IT. FOLLOW ME.

COME INTO THE GARDEN SHED, SID.

SOON...

RIGHT, SID, GIVE IT THE OLD COWBOY DIVE ONTO THE BACK OF THAT HORSE!

O-OKAY!

EH? NO FEAR!

OOPS! TRUST THE HORSE TO TROT OFF AT A VITAL MOMENT!

HEE! HEE!

YOWF!

SPLAT!

TROT!

OKAY, GIDDY-UP, HOSS!

WOW! FAME AT LAST! I'VE BEEN ENTERED FOR A RODEO!

BAH! IT'S SO SMALL, MY FEET ARE STILL ON THE GROUND!

HOO! HOO!

YAHOO! LET'S GO! CHARGE!

RIGHT. ON YOU GO, SID! YOUR AUDIENCE AWAITS!

RIDE 'IM, COWBOY! ARE YOU SURE THIS'LL WORK, WILLIE?

HAR! I ALWAYS KNEW MY OLD BUCKLED BIKE WOULD MAKE A BETTER BUCKING BRONCO!

YEE-HAH! MAGIC FIXIT, WILLIE.

BOUNCE!

BOING!

BONK!

The NEALS on WHEELS

GOOD LUCK AT THE GYMKHANA, HORTENSE.

GYMKHANA and HORSE TRIALS TODAY

PA NEAL K MA NEAL

KNOWN AS "HORSEY" FOR SHORT!

ER, I'M NOT TOO HEAVY FOR HIM, I HOPE.

SILLY GIRL — SHE'LL GET THROWN OFF, OR SOMETHING.

MUNCH!

GRANDMA NEAL

WHAT A LOVELY HORSE YOU ARE — BUT YOU'RE AWFULLY FRISKY.

LET'S GET GOIN'!

WOAH! STOP!

EH? WOT'S UP?

SCREECH!

THAT'S FAR TOO HIGH A JUMP FOR YOU! I'LL JUMP OVER IT INSTEAD.

EH?

STOP! STOP! I WON'T ALLOW YOU TO JUMP OVER THAT WATER! YOU MIGHT GET WET!

KUCKOO KOURT

PRISONER IN THE DOCK, YOU ARE ACCUSED OF STEALING A PENCIL. HOW DO YOU PLEAD?

GUILTY!

FOURTEEN YEARS IN JAIL! WITH YOU REALLY BAD CRIMINALS, WE'VE GOT TO **DRAW THE LINE** SOMEWHERE!

HO! HO! HO!

DONK!

JURY

NEXT CASE—

THE PRISONER STOLE A BUS AND REFUSED TO PICK UP ANY PASSENGERS, MY LORD.

TWENTY YEARS . . .

. . . THE TROUBLE WITH CRIMINALS LIKE YOU IS **YOU DON'T KNOW WHEN TO STOP!**

ORDER IN COURT!

HO! HO! HAW! HAW!

DONK!

FIVE COFFEES, SEVEN TEAS, A PACKET OF CHOCCY BICCIES . . .

HEE! HEE! A GROCERY ORDER!

YOU'RE OUT OF ORDER!

BONK!

POTTY INVENTIONS

THE COMPLETE COMPANION FOR DESERT ISLAND DICK!

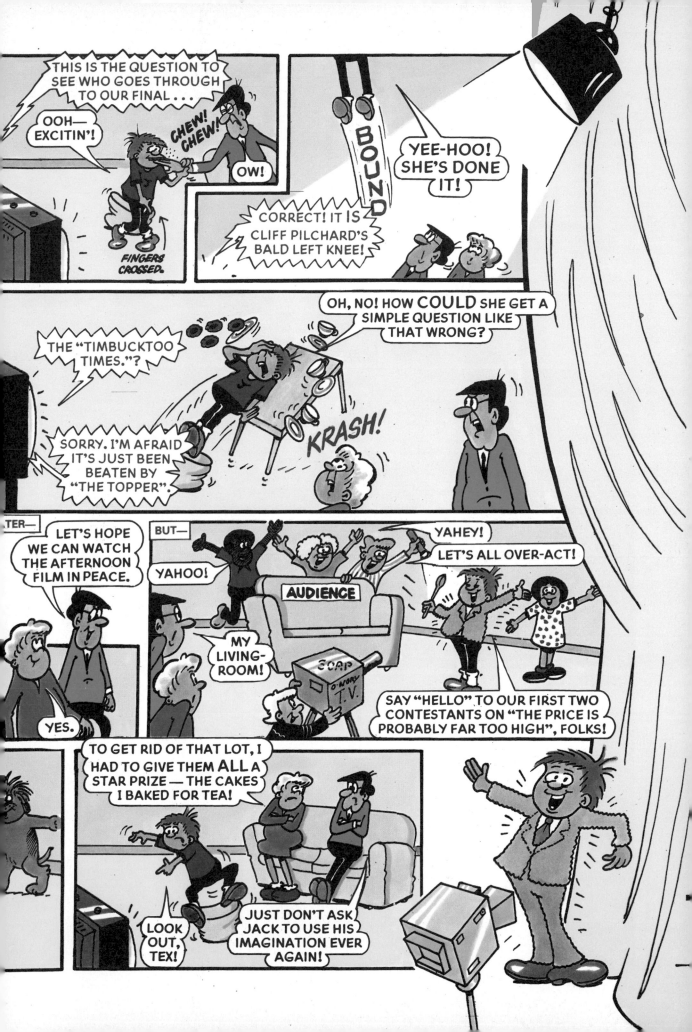

SOUPER BOY

A BIG CHANGE COMES OVER SOPPY SIDNEY BRAITHWAITE WHEN HE TAKES A SWIG OF HIS SOUPER-SOUP!

PHEW! IT'S HARD WORK PULLING MY SLEDGE! PUFF! I CAN'T GO ANY HIGHER UP THE SLOPE THAN THIS!

POW!

KAZAM!

WHOOM!

...BECOME SOUPER BOY!

THE FIRST THING A SOUPER BOY NEEDS IS A SOUPER SLEDGE!

GERROUTOVIT, YOU SOUPER MENACE!

HEY, SOUPER BOY — I'VE GOT SOMEWHERE YOU CAN USE YOUR SLEDGE — AND GET PAID FOR IT!

EH?

SOON, AT ROTTEN ROW —

SMASH!

JOE THE JANNY

9 A.M. —

PHUT! PHUT!

DRRRRAT!

IN YOU GO, KIDS . . . HULLO. WHAT'S THAT?

BROKEN DOWN, SIR? LEAVE IT TO ME. I'M GOOD WITH ENGINES.

FIFTEEN MINUTES LATER —

RUNNING SMOOTHLY AGAIN, THANKS TO YOU. IF YOU EVER NEED ANY HELP, HERE'S MY CARD.

NO TROUBLE, SIR . . . ER, EXCUSE ME!

I'M LATE!

PURR!

I'LL TRY T' SNEAK YOU INTO CLASS, BRIAN.

TA, JOE!

WHAT CAN I DO FOR YOU, JONES?

I'M JUST CHECKING THAT THE ROOM'S THE RIGHT TEMPERATURE, SIR.

SNORFT! I'VE GOT DUST UP ME NOSE FROM JOE'S JACKET.

WHASSAT?

ER, MUST BE A BIT CHILLY. THE — ER — DOOR'S CAUGHT A COLD.

ACHOO!

TIP-TOE!

BRIAN CLARK! YOU'RE LATE!

ULP! YOU NOTICED, SIR!

LATER — ...AND THE POOR LAD'S BEEN KEPT IN TO DO LINES. CAN YOU COME ROUND AND HELP HIM OUT? GOOD!

AT 4 P.M. — HOWDO, SIR! SO GLAD YOU COULD COME!

ONLY TOO GLAD TO HELP, JOE!

'SCUSE US, SIR!

EH?

TAP-TAP!

WHAT D'YOU WANT, JANITOR?

LIFT!

I'VE GOT A FRIEND HERE I'D LIKE YOU TO MEET, SIR. HE'S DOING AN ACT AT THE GLOBE THEATRE.

LOOK INTO MY EYES! YOU FEEL SLEEPY. YOU WILL OBEY MY INSTRUCTIONS!

I W-WILL OBEY YOUR INSTRUCTIONS!

SOON — THANKS FOR DEALING WITH TEACHER AND SHOWING US YOUR HYPNOTISING ACT, MISTER MYSTO!

HI, BRIAN!

ANYTIME, JOE! HEH!

HOWDO, ALL!

I WILL DO ALL BRIAN'S LINES ... I WILL DO ALL BRIAN'S LINES ...

DANNY'S TRANNY

YOUNG Danny Wilson owns a super-marvellous transistor radio. With it, he can make objects larger, smaller, lighter than air or even invisible! However, the fantastic effects of the tranny's rays last for only a short time.

CHARGE!

BANG! BANG! GOT YOU, DANNY.

WE'LL COVER YOU, DANNY.

ON THE TOWN DUMP DANNY AND FRIENDS ARE "ON MANOEUVRES"!

OH, RATS! IT'S STARTING TO RAIN.

LOOK! AN OLD BROLLY.

HOW'S THAT?

GROWING RAY LWIS

SUPER! YOUR TRANNY'S JUST MAGIC.

BUT—

WOW! THE WIND'S CAUGHT THE BROLLY.

WE'RE PARATROOPERS NOW — OOW!

THEN—

YEEPS! THE BROLLY'S COLLAPSED!

WE'RE IN FOR A PROPER BUMP!

GIANTS OF THE PAST

TYRANNOSAURUS — This savage brute was nearly 20 feet high.

DIMETRODON — A fierce lizard that lived in swamps. It was about 10 feet long.

TICHORHINUS — A kind of rhinoceros with a furry coat. It was 6 feet high and 12 feet long.

STEGOSAURUS — 25 feet long and 9 feet high. Its spiky tail was the terror of its enemies.

PTERODACTYL — A huge, flying reptile with a wing-span of 25 feet.

GLYPTODON — 12 feet long and 5 feet high. This odd beast was protected by its hard, bony covering.

MAMMOTH — Something like a present-day elephant, but with a shaggy coat and much larger tusks. About 13 feet high.

TRICERATOPS — Although this creature was about 25 feet long, its brain was no bigger than a kitten's.

PROTOCERATOPS — This lizard with the strangely-shaped head grew to a length of about 6 feet.

DIPLODOCUS — This was the biggest of them all. When fully grown it was over 80 feet long.

DESERT ISLAND DICK

GOSH! LOOK AT THAT HUGE BOX! BUT IT'S SURROUNDED BY SHARKS.

I'VE GOT TO RISK IT. IT'S BOUND TO BE FULL OF FOOD.

WHEE! YOU CAN'T AFFORD TO HANG ABOUT WITH SHARKS ON YOUR TRAIL.

ZOOM!

MADE IT! NOW LET'S SEE WHAT'S INSIDE.

ARGH!

SNAP!

GNASH!

TO LONDON AQUARIUM

YEEPS! ISLAND, HERE I COME.

BAH! BLOOMIN' SHARKS!

THE VIDEO KID IN THE WIZARD OF OOZE!

ANYWAY, LET'S GET ON WITH THE STORY!

HO-HUH! MY NAME'S DOROTHY, AN' MY HOUSE HAS BEEN CAUGHT UP IN A WHIRLWIND.

BLOW!

I DON'T HALF FEEL DAFT! THE THINGS I DO FOR THIS FILM COMPANY!

SAY "CHEESE".

I 'S'POSE I'D BETTER ACT THIS OUT WITH A BIT OF SPINNING OF MY OWN.

SPIN!

Y'WOT? THIS WASN'T IN THE SCRIPT!

FLASH!

WONDERWOMAN? WOT IS THIS?

FILM COSTUMIER

WELL, SHE DOES THAT SPINNING BIT TO CHANGE, SO I THOUGHT YOU'D DECIDED TO PLAY AT BEING HER!

TOSS!

LET'S GET ON WITH THE FILM, SHALL WE? I WONDER WHERE I'VE LANDED?

YOU'RE ON OZ . . . HEY! NO! THIS IS OOZE! WE'RE IN THE WRONG STORY!

THEN —

WE'RE THE ELVES, AND YOU'VE FLATTENED THE WICKED WITCH OF THE WEST AND DONE US A BIG FAVOUR.

USELESS ACTORS!

SEND FOR **KELLY**

AND HIS ASSISTANT **CEDRIC**

IN THE CASE OF

THE SOARING SNATCHER.

I MUST CHECK THE DOOR BEFORE WE LEAVE, ELSIE.

YOU CAN'T BE TOO CAREFUL.

SUDDENLY— SNATCH!

EEK! MY MINK COAT!

PRESENTLY, AT KELLY'S PLACE—

WHAT'S THAT, MINISTER? SOMEONE'S PINCHED YOUR WIFE'S FUR-COAT? WE'LL BE OVER RIGHT AWAY.

THIS IS WHERE THE SNATCH WAS MADE.

BOO-HOO!

MOST ODD! NO CLUES — NOT EVEN FOOTPRINTS.

LATER, AT KELLY'S AUNT FREDA'S FLAT—

EEK! MY PEARLS! STOP, THIEF!

SHORTLY—

...A HAND CAME THROUGH THE WINDOW.

WE'LL LOOK INTO THIS, AUNTIE.

ANOTHER MYSTERY! NO TELL-TALE FOOTPRINTS LEFT IN THE SNOW.

LATER—

COME ON, CEDRIC. A THIEF HAS JUST SWIPED COUNTESS TARA'S TIARA.

NICK KELLY SPECIAL AGENT

THREE ROBBERIES IN ONE NIGHT. PHEW!

I WAS STANDING HERE FEEDING THE DICKIE-BIRDS WHEN MY TIARA WAS SNATCHED! YET THERE WAS NOBODY TO BE SEEN.

AND AS USUAL— NO FOOTPRINTS.

THE THIEF MUST BE MAKING HIS GETAWAY OVER THE ROOF-TOPS, MISTER KELLY.

GOOD THINKING, CEDRIC. LET'S GO UP AND INVESTIGATE.

WE MIGHT FIND SOME CLUES ON THE FLAT ROOF UP HERE.

FUNNY! A CIRCLE OF MELTED SNOW.

HMM! I THINK THE ROBBER IS USING SOME KIND OF FLYING MACHINE.

WE CAN SEE FOR MILES FROM UP HERE.

AND I CAN USE OUR PORTABLE LISTENING DEVICE.

SUFFERIN' CATFISH!

LOOK! A HOT-AIR BALLOON — AND IT'S COMING THIS WAY.

JUMP ABOARD, CEDRIC. THIS COULD BE OUR THIEF.

LEAP!

YIPPEE! OUR WEIGHT'S FORCING IT DOWN.

BUT WHEN THE BALLOON LANDS, ITS GONDOLA TURNS OUT TO BE A DETACHABLE BUBBLE-CAR!

HE'S GOT AWAY BEFORE WE COULD STOP HIM.

LATER—

RIGHT, THEN — WE'RE ALL SET TO SURPRISE THAT CROOK IF HE TRIES TO STRIKE AGAIN.

SMART IDEA OF YOURS, THIS, MISTER KELLY.

SOON—

THERE HE IS, CEDRIC! DROP YOUR WEIGHTS. YAHOO! WE HAVE LIFT-OFF.

RIGHT, CEDRIC — OPEN FIRE!

GOT HIM!

HO! HO! NO CHANCE OF HIM USING HIS BUBBLE-CAR THIS TIME. IT'S SOMEWHAT DENTED!

FLOMP!

GOSH! THE CROOK'S NOT A MAN AT ALL — IT'S GREEDY-GRAN!

THE FAMOUS ARCH-VILLAINESS! WHAT'S THAT SHE'S GOT?

I'LL TEACH THOSE MEDDLESOME 'TECS A LESSON.

MORE POTTY INVENTIONS

A TABLE FOR FATTIES!

A DOOR MAT FOR UNFRIENDLY NEIGHBOURS!

SELF-DRAINING WELLIES!

A ONE-ARMED BANDIT FOR HUNGRY HORACE!

SLIMMERS' SCALES FOR MUMS!

A SPOON FOR NASTY-TASTING MEDICINE!

FOOTBALL CRAZY

PEARL

PEARL MUST BE IN A GOOD MOOD! SHE'S COMING TO MEET ME.

WHY DON'T YOU DO SOMETHING **USEFUL** — LIKE CLEARING AWAY THE SNOW?

OKAY.

AGGH!

HOW'S THAT?

DIG! DIG! DIG!

HEY — NOT SO FAST, YOU DAFT DOG!

YIPPEE! THIS IS MORE LIKE IT!

PICKING UP SPEED.

SOON—

HEH! LOOK AT DAD NOW —

TRICKY DICKY

JUST WHAT I'VE BEEN WAITING FOR — SNOW! THE MINI-SNOW-PLOUGHS ARE OUT.

PUTT!

BUT WAIT TILL YOU SEE MINE IN ACTION!

SHOVEL!

JUST WATCH THE DIFFERENT WAYS I'VE GOT TO MOVE SNOW.

YAK! YAK!

FIRST OF ALL, THERE'S TENNIS SNOW!

FLIP!

BLAH! BLAH!

AN ACE! HEE! HEE!

BLATT!

BLUP!

ALI'S BABA

THE BABE WITH THE INVISIBLE BODYGUARD

HAS BABA GOT SIX BLOCKS, OR SEVEN? IT ALL DEPENDS HOW YOU LOOK AT IT.

TOM AND TERRY'S CHUM LOOKS BIGGER THAN THEY DO, BUT IF YOU MEASURE THEM, YOU'LL FIND THEY'RE ALL THE SAME HEIGHT!

OPTICAL

HOLD THE BOOK ABOUT A FOOT FROM YOUR FACE AND CLOSE YOUR LEFT EYE. AS YOU WATCH THE CROSS ON THE MAGICIAN'S WAND, AND BRING THE BOOK TOWARDS YOU, THE BLACK SPOT ON THE RIGHT WILL DO A VANISHING TRICK!

IF YOU HOLD THE BOOK LEVEL WITH YOUR EYES, AND MOVE IT ROUND IN CIRCLES, YOU'LL SEE PA NEAL SPIN HIS STEERING WHEEL!

IT LOOKS LIKE THERE ARE GREY DOTS BETWEEN THE CORNERS OF THE SQUARES ON MISTER FAT-TUM'S WAISTCOAT. BUT IF YOU STARE AT ANY ONE DOT, IT WILL DISAPPEAR!

IS FIGARO LOOKING AT A COIL OF WIRE STANDING UPRIGHT, OR LYING ON ITS SIDE? BOTH, IT WOULD SEEM!

THE SIDES OF THE BADGE ON THIS PIRATE'S HAT SEEMS TO BE BENT. BUT YOU CAN'T BELIEVE YOUR EYES! THEY'RE REALLY QUITE STRAIGHT!

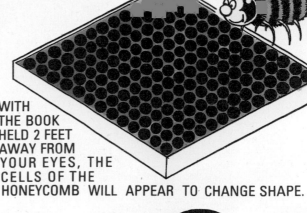

WITH THE BOOK HELD 2 FEET AWAY FROM YOUR EYES, THE CELLS OF THE HONEYCOMB WILL APPEAR TO CHANGE SHAPE.

ONE OF THIS CHAP'S EYES SEEMS TO BE BIGGER THAN THE OTHER, BUT THEY'RE THE SAME SIZE.

IS THAT A DUCK STARING PEARL IN THE FACE — OR IS PEARL LOOKING AT THE BACK OF A RABBIT'S HEAD?

LD THIS PICTURE ABOUT AN INCH FROM YOUR NOSE FOR A SHORT ME, AND SEE THE "BERYL BALLOON" FLY TOWARDS THE HOUSE!

THESE FUNNY-LOOKING MEN APPEAR TO BE LEANING OVER. BUT CHECK, AND YOU'LL FIND THAT THEY'RE STANDING PERFECTLY UPRIGHT.

WHICH END MUST POLLY PULL TO GET THE ARROW OUT? YOU'LL BE SURPRISED WHEN YOU USE A RULER TO FIND OUT.

SILLY TWIT! YOU MISSED!

DO A "PRETEND" TRIP AND GRAB THE BEARD, JIM!

PRETEND TRIP!

STILL WANT TO FIND OUT? CLIMB ON TOP OF THE GROTTO.

Santa's Grotto

NOW LEAN OVER AND PULL HIS BEARD OFF!

YIKES!

OORF!

WHUMP!

STUPID, STUPID, STUPID, BOY! GRAAAGH!

BONK!

BAH! YOU WERE BOTH WRONG — IT'S NOT THE REAL SANTA, OR NICE MR. WILKINS . . . IT'S BAD-TEMPERED MR GRUMPLEY!